PRAISE FOR BOB MCCALL AND
ZERO ACCIDENTS & INJURIES

"I have known Bob McCall more than thirty years. He is one of the best safety leaders I have ever worked with. He has a unique skill that motivates and excites individuals and teams to perform at industry-leading safety levels. This gift is not one of programs, threats, and rules, but he seems to capture the hearts and minds of people, and more importantly, he incites a passion to work safely and to help others around you to work safely. You and your team will benefit from Bob's leadership, passion, and approach to a safe workplace. I sure did."

—Lloyd M. Yates, senior executive, utilities industry

"Bob McCall was an exceptional guest speaker for our company summit. He was enjoyable to work with, and we were beyond pleased with his audience interaction and his enthusiasm about leadership and workplace safety. He picked up on our company culture quickly and made us all think a little more about what we can do to create a positive work environment every single day."

—Larissa Barbee, marketing coordinator/recruiter, Colt Builders Corporation

"The first time I talked to Bob McCall was on the phone and instantly, I had to meet him and learn more about his passion for excellence, especially in safety. That face-to-face meeting in 2003 provided me a front-seat and deep insight into one of the greatest safety leaders I have ever worked with. His messages on safety are clear, direct, and drive right to the root of the issues, and his delivery methods create an environment of confidence and personal commitment to achieve safety excellence. If you are seeking to move your team's safety performance from a culture of compliance to conviction, this is the book to read."

—John Smith, senior vice president, delivery operations, utilities industry

ZERO

ACCIDENTS & INJURIES

ZERO

ACCIDENTS & INJURIES

ARE YOU WILLING TO PAY THE PRICE?

BOB McCALL

Advantage®

Published by Advantage, Charleston, South Carolina.
Member of Advantage Media Group.

ADVANTAGE is a registered trademark and the Advantage colophon is a trademark of Advantage Media Group, Inc.

Printed in the United States of America.

ISBN: 978-1-59932-731-0
LCCN: 2016948661

Cover design by George Stevens.

Advantage Media Group is proud to be a part of the Tree Neutral® program. Tree Neutral offsets the number of trees consumed in the production and printing of this book by taking proactive steps such as planting trees in direct proportion to the number of trees used to print books. To learn more about Tree Neutral, please visit **www.treeneutral.com.**

Advantage Media Group is a publisher of business, self-improvement, and professional development books. We help entrepreneurs, business leaders, and professionals share their Stories, Passion, and Knowledge to help others Learn & Grow. Do you have a manuscript or book idea that you would like us to consider for publishing? Please visit **advantagefamily.com** or call **1.866.775.1696.**

I would like to dedicate this book to my mom, who believed I could do great things. Her love, friendship, and dedication were demonstrated throughout her life and during her illness, an attitude very inspirational to me.

TABLE OF CONTENTS

ACKNOWLEDGMENTS

I must start out by thanking God for the talents he's given me and the life experiences that have enabled me to share this process that can bring about top performance in safety, thus saving lives. I want to thank Jesus Christ for being my Lord and Savior and providing the guide for how life should be lived. To my wife, Benita, for her awesome love and support. To my daughters, Chandell and Shanena, remember, "You can do all things through Christ who strengthens you" (Philippians 4:13). I'm very thankful to my parents, Bob and Geraldine McCall, for the sacrifice they made sending me to private schools to ensure I got the best education and for the love, support, and wisdom they passed down. Special love to Mom, who died at fifty-six. Her dedication and inspiration were second to none.

I'd also like to give big shout-outs to the following:

- My sister Andrida, who is an awesome actor, director, and teacher; my brother-in-law Boyzell, who is an awesome photographer and leader; Uncle Josh and Aunt Celeste, who have been like parents to me, thanks for always being there; and Uncle Will and Aunt Nancy, for providing my sister and I with some of the most memorable experiences that helped shape our lives.

- Robert and Gloria Mungin, whose inspiration and belief in me help drive me, and their son and one of my best friends, Bob Mungin Jr., who always had my back.

- "My gang": Keith and Lavern Clark, Fats (Art) and Dawn Nance, Bob and Carla Mungin, Corey Swanson, Chris and Jane Gubernot, Kelly O'Rourke, John and Brenda Low, Ken and Trace Davis, Ray and Pattie Livingston, Rufus and Monique Bynum, Jeff and Alice Carney, Jackie Boatwright-Stroop, and Ted and Michelle Stout.

- My Canadian crew: Rob and Bonnie Sharp and Terry and Barb Farlow. They and their families provide me love and support during my time in Michigan.

- Ben Carter, my big brother, and the Carter family. Ben was a great role model for me. A man with character, and strong beliefs. Ben, I can't thank you enough for your constant belief in me.

• The pastors in my life whose spiritual guidance and education inspired me. Pastor James Toney and the Shekinah Glory family got me started in fulfilling my Christian walk. He believed in me and allowed me to function in many areas of ministry. Pastor Frank Dawson and the Alpha and Omega family. He took my spiritual education to another level and also allowed me to serve in many areas of his ministry. Pastor Robert Campbell and the New Beginning family. His high energy, can-do attitude, and belief in me right off the bat allowed me to begin serving his great church. Pastor Troy and Pastor Penny Maxwell and the Freedom House family's love for all people is driving me now.

• Leroy Dillard, who told me at age fifteen that I had "something special," a call on my life. Leroy, I can't thank you enough for your constant belief in me. Your wisdom, talent, and passion are second to none.

• Lloyd Yates, for being a brother, a great friend, and a mentor who always believed in me and gave me many significant professional opportunities to shine. Thank you for always believing in me.

- My many friends and family who believed in and supported me along the way.

I couldn't have done it without you guys.

FOREWORD

Several years ago I attended a company-sponsored event. The main speaker was full of enthusiasm and had a knack for engaging the audience. Throughout the presentation he continued to engage and encourage everyone in the auditorium to embrace his message. There was no doubt how much passion he had for his presentation material. I was so impressed with the speaker that I introduced myself after the meeting and told him I wanted to be on his team one day.

It was just a few short years later that I in fact joined his team. I was very excited to be part of a team so focused on accomplishing a mission. That mission was to create a world-class safety organization. That speaker, Robert "Bob" McCall, had become my mentor. He understood that in order to achieve excellence in safety, you had to first create the desire in the people. You can have the best work safety practices and extremely detailed procedures available to facilitate a safe work environment, but in the end, each and every employee must choose to follow them. Bob built that desire through his human-performance culture and worked toward the goal of leaving no one behind.

Bob's success came because he cared. He truly cared for each individual. He strove to know everyone on the team and to help him or her nurture the desire from within. However, in every organization there are those who require a more direct approach. Bob possesses the ability to hold individuals accountable and meet issues head-on. He is skilled in conflict management and finds quick resolutions to issues.

Bob has a vast history of creating strong safety and human-performance cultures everywhere he goes. It is a way of life, not a safety program, that Bob brings to the table.

—Ray Livingston
Director of field services, East, PowerGrid Engineering, LLC

ABOUT THE AUTHOR

ROBERT HAMILTON MCCALL JR. is the president of Inspire High Performance, LLC, a Charlotte, North Carolina-based motivational-speaking and corporate-training firm that teaches companies and organizations how to build a culture of high safety performance in which everyone can work at their top potential every day, thus saving lives, preventing injuries, recognizing errors, and improving processes. An energetic and engaging motivational speaker, McCall shares the proven techniques he developed throughout his vast experience in the energy industry on how to successfully turn around underperforming operations and functions. He never fails to challenge the status quo and inspire his audiences to reach for the next level of safety performance within their own organizations.

A native of Pittsburgh, Pennsylvania, McCall graduated from Central Catholic High School and then attended Tuskegee

University, where he earned a bachelor's degree in Building Technology (construction). McCall began his career in the energy industry with Bechtel Power Corporation, working on construction, maintenance, and operations for nuclear power plants for ten years. McCall left Bechtel to begin his career with Iowa Electric (now Alliant Energy) at the Duane Arnold Energy Center in Palo, Iowa.

After seven years with Alliant, McCall became the first African American plant manager at Progress Energy's H. F. Lee Power Plant, located in Goldsboro, North Carolina. A year later, he was promoted to general manager for the Eastern region fossil generation department, becoming responsible for five plants, traveling maintenance, engineering, and project management. Later, McCall moved to the transmission department, where he served as the general manager of asset management; then to distribution, where he served as the general manager of the Southern Region; and then to vice president of the Eastern region in energy delivery, where he was responsible for thirteen operation centers serving 350,000 customers. In 2011, Progress Energy merged with Duke Energy, the largest electric power holding company in the United States, with assets in Canada and Latin America. Duke Energy's more than 250,000 miles of distribution lines serve some 7.1 million customers. [1]

---

1 Mike Hughes, Duke Energy, January 29, 2013, http://www.duke-energy.com/news/releases/2013012901.asp.

Next, McCall was named general manager of Fleet Services at Duke Energy, a position that was responsible for managing over thirteen thousand vehicles and pieces of mobile equipment valued at over $800 million, operating in fifty-eight locations across six states. After thirty-three years in the energy industry, McCall retired from Duke Energy. Today, he follows his passion of teaching energy companies and other organizations how to inspire higher safety performance in all their employees.

McCall has had the opportunity to take his message to a number of groups across the nation. They include conferences throughout the United States, Tucson Electric, Hawaii Electric, the Canadian Utility Fleet Council, Incident Prevention, Sea Box, and Captive workshops.

To find out more about Bob McCall's unique approach to improving safety performance or to engage him as a keynote speaker at your next event, please contact him using the following information.

INSPIRE HIGH PERFORMANCE, LLC

INFO@INSPIREHIGHPERFORMANCE.COM

INSPIREHIGHPERFORMANCE.COM

C- 910-520-7371

INTRODUCTION

"If better is possible,
then good is no longer an option."

Kenston Griffin,
Dream Builders Communication, Inc.

First thing I want you to know is you *can* do this! Everyone has greatness inside them. Let me show you how to tap into your power so that, together, we can protect our team members and ourselves from future accidents and injuries.

My vision for safety performance across any industry is simple: ZERO first aid cases, ZERO recordable injuries, ZERO lost-time accidents, ZERO fatalities, and ZERO controllable vehicle accidents and incidents. I can almost hear the groans and see the eyes rolling from all you skeptics out there regarding my bold use of the word *zero*. During my early years working in the power industry, I too believed that accidents and injuries were an inevitable part of the job. Then one day an accident occurred that hit too close to home. That incident made me start questioning everything I thought I knew about on-the-job safety.

On September 4, 1985, I was part of the crew completing construction of the Hope Creek Nuclear Generating Station in Alloways Creek, New Jersey. Hope Creek is a thermal nuclear power plant located on the same site as the Salem Nuclear Power Plant. Today, the Salem-Hope Creek complex is the largest nuclear generating facility in the eastern United States and the second largest in the nation.

The day began like many others, though all of the three thousand workers at the site were feeling the final push to get the facility completed and ready to go online in the summer of 1986. Then, at 8:45 a.m., disaster struck. The alarm bells sounded when an accidental release of carbon dioxide from an automatic fire-suppression system occurred inside a diesel generating room and adjacent fuel-storage room. I rushed to the location to see if I could assist the emergency medical crews with first aid. As I arrived, the first person I saw being carried out of the facility on a stretcher was my dear friend and future roommate. As I reached his side, my mind was flooded with many questions. How did this happen? What would I say to his mother if he didn't make it? What would I tell his brother, who also works in the industry? And the most nagging questions of all: Could this accident have been prevented?

By the end of that difficult day, twenty-one people had been hospitalized with breathing problems stemming from carbon dioxide poisoning, with one in critical condition; fifty other workers had been treated at the scene. One accident. Seventy-one victims.

Even as my friend and other fellow workers recovered and returned to work, I continued to wrestle with that disturbing question: Could the accident have been prevented?

The Hope Creek Nuclear Generating Station went online in July 1986. By 1992, I had finished out my construction career and accepted a position as a planner (later being promoted to mechanical maintenance supervisor) at Duane Arnold Energy Center in Palo, Iowa. Built in 1974, it is the only nuclear power plant in Iowa.

In my new supervisory role, I was fortunate to attend human-performance training in Atlanta offered by the Institute of Nuclear Power Operations (INPO), an organization that exists to promote the highest levels of safety and reliability in the operation of commercial nuclear power plants across the nation. It was during that training that I had the good fortune to hear Tony Muschara speak. The principal consultant and owner of Muschara Error Management Consulting, he is an expert in the field of human performance.

During the training, Muschara explained that the study of human behavior reveals that errors are predictable, manageable, and *preventable*. I finally had the answer to the question that had plagued me since the accident at Hope Creek. And the answer was *yes*! That answer changed my life.

I left that INPO training knowing that workers across the power industry could work every day, free from accidents and injuries. That did it for me. That truth lit my passion to learn everything I could about how safety leaders just like you and me can work to prevent *all* on-the-job first aid cases, recordable injuries, lost-time accidents, fatalities, and controllable vehicle accidents and incidents.

Prior to the INPO training in Atlanta, I had attended a seminar in San Francisco featuring Chong Chiu, PhD, who founded Performance Improvement International in 1987 with the goal of improving safety and performance in the nuclear power industry. His body of work, coupled with Muschara's, fueled my passion to take safety performance to a higher level in my workplace and in my industry. I began reading everything I could get my hands on regarding human performance and related fields.

Eager to prevent accidents and injuries at work, I began implementing various strategies I'd learned into my work environment and observing the real-life effects. Based on the results I observed, I began refining my strategies to achieve maximum results. I did this by incorporating the best of what I'd learned from the human-performance experts with what I'd discovered on my own during my many years working in the industry. I've used these powerful strategies in different locations with different people, both union and nonunion, professionals and technicians. Once I knew for sure that I had a proven process that always yielded success—it worked every time it was tried—I knew it was time to get these strategies into the hands of other safety leaders. Why was this so important to me? At the time, I was the mechanical maintenance supervisor of twenty-five fantastic people whom I loved and appreciated very much. I now had information that could protect them and their families. Why wouldn't I share it? Knowledge is power when it's shared.

In 2008, I began sharing these strategies through presentations and keynote addresses to safety leaders in the power and utility industries across the country. I still get excited when I receive e-mails, phone calls, or run into former conference attendees letting me know that they tried one or more of the strategies I suggested and it worked. For me, helping people stay safe on the job is what's it's all about.

What about you? As a leader who is responsible for the safety of your workers, what legacy do you want to leave behind when your role changes, you move on, or you retire? If your answer is to leave behind a couple more volumes of safety rules, I urge you to rethink your goals. Of course safety rules are necessary, but piling on more and more seldom has a positive effect on a company's safety statistics. So if you were hoping for a few well-worded safety rules here that would magically get your safety performance to the next level, you've come to the wrong place.

Having a positive, sustainable impact on safety at your company begins with leadership—your leadership. It takes the kind of leadership that will change the hearts and minds of all your team members—the kind of leadership that will get them to buy in to the company's vision and goals for safety and make them their own. With this book in hand, you'll know how to do that regardless of your personal leadership style.

My vision for safety performance across industries is achievable: ZERO first aid cases, recordable injuries, lost-time accidents, fatalities, and controllable vehicle accidents and incidents. It's a vision that's achievable for every safety leader in the power and other industries, including you. Are you willing to pay the price? Are you willing to challenge long-term relationships of people who have behaviors that are destroying your team's performance? Are you willing to set challenging expectations? Are you willing to hold people accountable? Are you willing to get out and meet your team—to build relations with them and find them doing things right? Are you willing to improve your leadership skills by learning best practices that really connect people? Are you willing to be the person your team can emulate? These are the prices for getting your team to the next level. I challenge you that the cost of doing nothing is much higher.

CHAPTER ONE

LEADERSHIP

CHAPTER 1: LEADERSHIP

*"To make something special you
just have to believe it's special."*

—Mr. Ping, *Kung Fu Panda*

I love the part of the story when Po (the titular Kung Fu Panda) realized he had the power to defeat the villain (Tai Lung) and that it was all wrapped up around his belief system. One rainy Saturday I found myself watching a *Kung Fu Panda* marathon. After watching it three times, I started taking notes and ended up with two pages of leadership notes. The pinnacle of the movie begins when Po realizes that the true power from all his training was wrapped up around him believing in himself. He had to be the one to get the team excited, energized, and confident that they could achieve. Po was the secret ingredient to get the team going. Leadership positions put us in the same situation. We are the secret ingredient—we must step up to the challenge if we want to see any improvement in our team's performance. When our team members see us excited, they will get excited. When they see us giving and caring more, they will start giving and caring more. You get the point: you are the secret ingredient!

If you knew there was a proven formula for achieving a higher level of safety performance for your team and your organization, would you use it? Maybe the more appropriate question is: Would you have the courage to use it? If your answer is *yes*, your journey begins with leadership.

Why does it start with leadership? Because being a leader is huge. In fact, it's the most important responsibility you will undertake in your work life. As a leader in any industry, you hold people's lives in your hands. Think about that for a moment. We have the power to build up or destroy careers. We have the power to motivate or isolate, promote or demote. We have the power (and responsibility) to get our team members and ourselves home every night, alive and free of injuries. I said it before, and I'll say it again—being a leader is huge! Someone saw something in you that made you stand out from the rest. Don't let them down! When I began my study of human performance in the late 1990s, and of leadership in the mid-1980s, I quickly realized that using all the research on how to get safety performance to a higher level in the workplace begins and ends with leadership.

Throughout my career as a leader, I've told other leaders, "Don't get into the leadership game to make more money." Trust me; there are easier ways to make money. But if you do decide to be a leader, you must like and care about the people with whom you work. The people you are responsible for must be the most important part of your leadership plan. You must also have a desire and belief that you can make a difference.

Unfortunately, too many leaders in our industry are in it strictly for the money and prestige, allowing others in their organizations to orchestrate the direction of their teams. They have no vision for the team or the department. They have no intention of trying to touch the lives of the team. Please don't be the kind of leader that people believe are just waiting on their next promotion.

Be the leader who believes he or she can make a difference and has a desire to connect with the team to motivate and encourage them. If this is you, here is the best definition I've found for leadership. It comes from Behavior Technologies, a company with four decades of experience helping people and organizations achieve high levels of performance and fulfillment.

WHAT IS A LEADER?

- A leader is able to influence the actions and opinions of others in a desired direction.
- A leader exhibits judgment in leading others to worthwhile objectives.
- A leader is able to assume a role of authority as necessary.
- A leader advocates for new ideas, even when risk is involved.
- A leader delegates responsibility and empowers associates to make decisions.
- A leader provides constructive feedback to others.
- A leader sets an example for others to emulate.

One of the principles I want to make sure you focus on is the third one: "able to assume a role of authority as necessary." Many leaders believe that it's their job to find people doing things wrong so they can correct them. I'm not saying that correction isn't proper at times; rather, I'm saying that you should try to find your people doing things "right." Find their strengths—the things they're good at. When you do, get excited about it, compliment them, praise them, and express how thankful you are to have them on the team. Make sure you're sincere. This behavior motivates people and makes them feel special, needed, and valued.

Here is an example (think about what you hear in this communication):

"Hey Jim, how are you doing today? How're Becky and the kids? How did your son's game turn out? Jim, I want you to know that every time I walk by your job sites, you have the most remarkable housekeeping practices. Your tools are always neatly placed where they won't be a tripping hazard to you or other team members. You always take the extra time to put up cones to mark the hazard areas, and you keep your truck just as organized. I want to start a Housekeeping team, and I would like you to consider being the leader Jim. Talk to Becky about the opportunity, and let me know tomorrow. The company would benefit by having someone as thorough as you leading the team.

What did you hear in my communication with Jim?

This is leadership. John Maxwell calls it "Believing in people before they prove themselves." Belief is a very powerful leadership tool. When you believe in people you transfer power and confidence that they can achieve. People become motivated and want to be engaged in forwarding the mission. People feel they can make a difference. All because you believed and supported them.

When you truly understand and embrace your important role as a leader, you understand that leaders own improvement. Leaders find ways to win, leaders get the ball rolling, leaders set the vision, and leaders set the expectations. I believe that you can make a difference in the safety performance in your workplace. I'm often asked, "Are leaders born or created?" My answer to that question is, "Both." I believe that some are born with a personality that includes many leadership qualities, but I also believe if you have a passion and want to be a great leader, there are many resources available to help you acquire the skills and attributes you need to lead. (You will find a list of some of my favorite resources in the back of the book). Here's something else to remember: all leadership styles work if you're sincere, genuine, respectable, and willing. But in order to make the kind of difference that will result in a higher level of performance in your workplace, you will likely have to make some changes in your thinking and your approach to leadership. Let's face it: we can't change other people. But people will change themselves, provided they are given the right knowledge, encouragement, motivation, and belief—all of which start with you as their leader.

ELEVATE YOUR LEADERSHIP

To elevate your leadership style, you must do something different than what's resulted in your current record of safety.

You get what you tolerate, so raise your standards, raise your expectations, and constantly work on improving your leadership skills. If you want your team members to change, you can't sit back and wait on them. You have to lead. The late, great Will Rogers once said, "Even if you're on the right track, you'll get run over if you just sit there." And Rev. Mary Omwake said, "Even God can't steer a parked car." The point is, great leaders are never standing still—they are always moving forward. So start studying leadership like a skill and never stop (again, see the list of leadership books in the back).

In all my years serving as a leader, I've found that the following four principles resonate across the board in every situation that involves human interaction.

1. "People achieve high levels of performance based largely on the **encouragement** and reinforcement received by leaders and peers." —James T. Reason, grandfather of human performance

2. "People work best for/with those who make them **feel good about themselves.**" —John C. Maxwell, author (His leadership books are some of my favorites.)

3. "You have to create an **encouraging culture** where the focus is on love, trust, commitment, and belief." —Lou Holtz, hall of fame college football coach

4. "You can't have excellence without *great teamwork*."
—Lou Holtz

I've tried these four principles in a number of energy industry environments, both union and nonunion. They are 100 percent true, and they work!

Once you've made the commitment to constantly work on your leadership skills, the first step toward the next level of safety performance in your workplace is a vision. For me, the vision is obvious and worth repeating here: ZERO first aid cases, ZERO recordable injuries, ZERO lost-time accidents, ZERO fatalities, and ZERO controllable vehicle accidents and incidents. When it comes to visions, I'm not one to let "good" keep me from achieving the "best" possible outcome for my team. It's bold in that it's the highest-possible result my team and I can achieve working together.

THE VISION

Zero:

- First Aid Cases!
- Recordable Injuries!
- Lost-Time Accidents!
- Fatalities!
- Controllable Vehicle Accidents!
- Incidents!

Using a sports analogy, professional sports teams don't start the season stating they want to be average or mediocre.

Their plan is to make the playoffs and go for the championship. Leaders must have a "winning" attitude.

John Maxwell says that people act differently when they sense a win, and he's right. He says people will get more engaged, make personal sacrifices to help the team, become energized, and look for more ways to help the team. People become motivated. Motivation is another powerful tool from leaders. I remember when I played strong safety on my high school football team. I blocked a field goal attempt in a very important game as a result of Coach Saloman believing in me and motivating me right before the play. He pulled me in, looked me directly in the eyes, and said, "Bobby, you can do this." I knew he loved me and believed in me, so I went out and jumped higher than I ever jumped before and blocked the field goal attempt. It turned the tempo of the game. The same can happen when your work team feels they can win from you. They will make big plays; they will go the extra mile for each other. It's like the TV commercial where a person witness another person doing something nice for someone. Now inspired, the person who witnessed the event goes and does something nice for another person, and the chain continues. This is what you as a leader can start by demonstrating the winning attitude, believing in your people, and being the first to say or do something nice for team members.

In leadership, there's always going to be someone who challenges your vision. You must stand strong. For example, when I would tell the team that I didn't want a scratch on anyone's body, someone would always challenge that statement, saying something like, "… Not a scratch?" to which I would reiterate my point, "Not a scratch." Then I would ask the question, "Tell me what job we ask you to do that there isn't one or more types of PPE (personal protective equipment) in the warehouse." Then the light went off in my team members' heads: *I guess we do have all we need to be protected.* "Thank you," I would say.

Note: This dialogue also allows you to demonstrate your care for every team member. I was able to make those statements about PPE because my company had proved its commitment to providing all that was needed to protect its people. This can be a revealing statement if you and your company don't have what it takes to protect your people. If you haven't made that commitment, you need to do it now. On the days when this vision seems daunting and unachievable, I encourage you to remember what Napoleon Hill, the author of *Think and Grow Rich*, once said: "Whatever the mind can conceive and believe, it can achieve."

GET IN THE GAME

How many more accidents do you need to see, hear about, read about, or investigate to make a change? If the answer is, "Not one more," then you're ready to lead your team to a higher level of safety performance. I am here to tell you that as leaders, we can, over time, achieve the ultimate in safety performance if we dare to keep our vision, belief and winning attitude in mind every day. After all, isn't it our responsibility as leaders to get every team member home to their families every day, alive and well? Once you've committed to your vision, the next step is to take it live—to start the process of convincing every member of your team to get on board. This is where the rubber meets the road.

Let me give you an example of how I got the ball rolling toward achieving the vision for my team. The last position I held before I retired was general manager of Fleet Services for the largest electric power holding company in the United States. I was responsible for managing over thirteen thousand vehicles and pieces of mobile equipment valued at over $800 million and operating in fifty-eight locations in six states.

I hit the road with the goal of introducing myself to all my leaders and teammates in every one of those fifty-eight locations. I put a lot of energy into those meetings. Leaders often struggle with the question, "How am I (a leader) supposed to appear to my team?" When I ask this question to leadership teams, I always get answers like "honest," "confident," "knowledgeable," and "humble." These answers are right but are not the first thing you want people to know. You want them to know that you are *human*—not better than them, not smarter than them—just like them. As Lou Holtz says, we all share one thing in common: problems. The next thing you want the team to know is that you are not the savior—you don't have all the answers. But together, there are many answers, and you need everyone involved and engaged. The team needs everyone's talents and skills to be the best team ever and to overcome whatever obstacles are to come.

Whenever possible, I'd take the team leaders from a location out to dinner, where I could engage each one of them. I had a series of messages that I shared with them to bond us quickly. These messages were simple things, like letting folks know right off the bat that even though we just met, I already liked them, respected them, and trusted them. I let them know that I appreciated them and that we were all working together trying to do the best we could to raise and support our families. That was our commonality. I let them know they didn't have to do anything to try to get me to like, respect, or trust them because I already did. When you share this message, people will relax and extend to you those same traits.

Then I went around the room and learned whatever I could from those leaders and team members. How long had they been in the industry? How did they get started in the industry? What did they like to do outside of the job? Did they have a spouse and/or children? When I got this level of engagement going, it was all about them. I think it's important for me to note that I didn't do this as an exercise. I genuinely care about the people working on my team, and I always do my best to remember what they tell me about themselves, such as their names and their histories in the industry. I also try to remember who likes to work out at the gym, who coaches their daughter's soccer team, and who loves to watch old movies on the weekends. Genuinely caring about people is hard to fake, so if you don't, you should not be in leadership.

Then I shared my message with the group. I shared my vision of ZERO first aid cases, recordable injuries, lost-time accidents, fatalities, and controllable vehicle accidents and incidents and began the process of getting them to embrace it, to make the

REQUIREMENTS TO GET TO THE NEXT LEVEL...

- Passion
- Care
- Leadership
- Drive
- Truth
- Courage
- Belief

vision their own. "What is your life worth?" I asked. "What are the lives of your team members worth? Are you sick and tired of injuries, short-term disabilities, long-term disabilities, and the types of attitudes that go with the kind of thinking that results in these injuries?" I explained the personal traits of leaders that would help get their teams to a higher level of safety performance. Those traits include passion, caring, leadership, drive, truth, courage, and belief.

At these initial meetings, I also laid the groundwork for the other topics I cover in this book, which include leadership, team culture, individual expectations, behaviors that cannot be tolerated, and hiring winners. As you make your way through these discussions, you will see the role leadership plays throughout the process of getting your company's safety performance to the next level. Without leadership—your leadership—the accidents and injuries that have been a persistent part of your industry for the last several decades will continue.

One last Leadership tip before I close the chapter. Don't take personal problems to work. Your team feeds off your energy weather it be positive or negative. If somethings going on and your can's shake it stay home till you can. I have an example that illustrates my point.

I remember one example when I pulled into the parking lot at work, and my wife called me on my cell phone. The first thing she said was, "Are you sitting down?" After I panicked and assured her that I was, she informed me that our teenage daughter had just gotten her third speeding ticket in a month—this one for going ninety-six miles an hour in a seventy-mile-an-hour zone. I went ballistic, yelling about the situation and thinking about exactly how I was going to handle it.

By now the windows were steaming up due to my anger when a colleague walked by and tapped on the driver's side window. "You all right in there, Bob?" she asked. I politely told my friend that my daughter just got her third speeding ticket in one month, and I was going to kill her.

Notice I did not take my anger out on my coworker. It wasn't her fault. I sat a few more minutes, took a few deep breaths, ratcheted down my punishment options (trading her beloved car for an old beater car and grounding her for life seemed about right), then mentally put my daughter's abominable driving record aside and went to work ready to motivate and inspire.

It's really no secret. Equipped with a vision, belief, a winning attitude, a plan for success, and leadership skills, you're what it takes to make accidents and injuries a thing of the past.

As we close the chapter, remember we're leaders. We must be the ones to get the ball rolling. We can't expect people to get it started if we're not on board. You can't motivate the people if you're not motivated.

"The best leaders are those who lead people to believe in themselves. People believe in themselves when they have a reason to commit to something significant and meaningful."

—Lolly Daskal, president and founder, Lead From Within (a consulting firm specializing in executive coaching and customized leadership programs)

Remember, you get what you tolerate.

TEAM CULTURE

CHAPTER 2: TEAM CULTURE

"People achieve high levels of performance based largely on the encouragement and reinforcement received from leaders, peers, and subordinates."

—James T. Reason, professor of psychology, University of Manchester

"People work best for those who make them feel good about themselves."

—John C. Maxwell, leading author in the study of leadership

"Culture trumps strategy every time. You need a plan, belief and a winning attitude. But without the team—the people backing that vision—it goes nowhere."

—Bob McCall, president, Inspire High Performance

Culture, culture, culture. The effects of setting the expectations for a powerful, high-performing culture was one thing I recognized many years ago, when I played high school and college football, ran track, and played baseball. The difference between a winning team and a losing team is not solely talent. As a matter of fact, it was often the case that the losing team had more talent than the winning team. But the losing team didn't have championship expectations; the team didn't respect each other; there was favoritism, no work ethic, and the coaches didn't agree and had power struggles. Winning or losing in sports is like winning or losing in life: you have the same participants—*people!*

Some principles for a winning culture are as follows:

- a loving environment with team members who show mutual respect

- a team willing to go the extra mile for each other

- trust in the team

- a team committed to the team, vision, and mission

- a team with members who believe in themselves, their team, and their leaders

When my daughter was in the third grade, I volunteered to coach her soccer team. I know quite a bit about football and baseball, having played both during my youth. I know a great deal about bodybuilding, and I can even give you a few pointers on how to get a fast car down the track without crashing. But soccer? I'd never played a game of soccer in my life. Thankfully, the other coach had some experience with the game!

So I headed off to a weekend-long coaching camp where we received sixteen hours of intensive training, a CD, and a book. On Monday afternoon at 5:30 p.m. sharp, I reported to the soccer field. I was officially a soccer coach. Believe me when I say that there is nothing on earth quite as intimidating as a bunch of enthusiastic eight-year-old and nine-year-old girls looking to you for guidance.

That team of third-grade girls went undefeated and won the championship that year. They didn't become the champions because I knew how to coach soccer, that's for sure.

Most of us have played on a sports team during our lifetimes. Having been on some winning teams as well as my share of losing teams, I thought for a long time about everything that goes into building a winning team versus a losing team. I recognized early on that it wasn't all about talent, because I'd seen a number of losing teams that were packed with talented players. The question continued to perplex me, so I looked for answers to that question in the materials I'd been studying since the 1990s about human performance.

After years of reading the research conducted by some of the top experts in the field, including Tony Muschara, Chong Chiu, James T. Reason, and others, I was able to draw on some of that knowledge. I also pulled on the knowledge I had experienced by being around some great coaches of teams I was on. I knew that first day on the field—surrounded by third graders—what I lacked in soccer expertise I could more than make up for with what I'd learned through the years about why some people achieve high levels of performance while others don't. That day, I had no idea if any of the girls were talented or experienced soccer players. But I knew without any doubt I was standing among champions. I believed in the girls before they proved themselves, and we had the winning attitude.

It's all about *team culture*—I remember what the great Coach Lou Holtz said: "You have to create an encouraging culture where the focus is on love, trust, commitment, and belief." It didn't take me long to see it with my own eyes; Holtz's philosophy not only works for sports teams, but it also works anywhere there are people involved. Heck, I even found that Holtz's principle works for overly excitable and easily distracted third-grade girls trying to move a soccer ball down the field. How do you create a high performing culture?—By encouragement and making them feel good about themselves! Remember the last chapter, when you start it, it becomes contagious. The goal is to get the team to encourage and make each other feel good about themselves.

Every day I spent coaching my daughter's soccer team was all about creating an encouraging team culture focused on love, trust, commitment, and belief. When a player kicked the ball correctly, we high-fived. When a player kicked it all wrong, we talked about how to fix it, followed by a high-five. When one of my girls made a great play during a game, I was shouting from the sidelines, "Way to go!" That was followed by a whole line of high-fives. I supported every member of that team with heavy doses of encouragement, and before long, they were supporting each other the same way. And the best part was that the better the team members felt about themselves, the better they performed on the field. Every player was eager to learn, eager to play, and eager to improve. Despite their coach's lack of experience and knowledge of soccer, together we created a team culture in which every player could perform at her highest level.

Of course, introducing the principles of love, trust, commitment, and belief to a bunch of sweet little girls is easy. Standing in front of a group of rough, tough, manly men who continue to dominate the front lines of the power industry is something else altogether. But I figured that if Coach Lou Holtz could introduce these principles into a football locker room, I'd give it my best shot, especially considering what was at stake. The lives of my team were in my hands.

By the time I was named general manager of Fleet Services, I had a formula for creating an encouraging team culture that would allow us to work toward achieving my vision of ZERO first aid cases, recordable injuries, lost-time accidents, fatalities, and controllable vehicle accidents and incidents. The first step was to get all the leaders across the fifty-eight locations I managed to buy in to my vision—to make it the entire team's vision.

As a leader, you must have the right team culture in the work environment to promote good safety behavior. But what will it take to change your team's safety culture? As a leader, you lead the way to a new team culture through your words and actions.

Through the years, I have developed a series of messages that are proven to move a team from a poor culture to an encouraging team culture—a team culture based on love, trust, commitment, and belief. These messages were an integral part of every safety meeting presentation I made during my early days as the general manager of Fleet Services, as well as in prior positions.

MESSAGE 1: "THERE'S NO JOB MORE IMPORTANT THAN YOU."

Think about what this is saying to your team. You value them more than any job or customer. Their families and loved ones matter to you. You don't want them to take any risks or shortcuts or break safety rules to be more productive. You value your team above all. Powerful words.

MESSAGE 2: "WE DON'T WANT TO SEE YOU HURT, AND WE'RE NOT GOING TO LET YOU HURT YOURSELF BY ALLOWING BEHAVIORS THAT WILL EVENTUALLY GET YOU HURT."

I love what this message says. Let's break it down. As a matter of fact, ask your team what they hear in this message. Ask them to dissect the message in two parts. Take the first part, "We don't want to see you hurt"...what do they hear in these words? What do they feel about these words? Then take the second, "and we're not going to let you hurt yourself by allowing behaviors that will eventually get you hurt." What does this part of the message say about the culture you have? How about the word "eventually"—does it mean you'll get hurt now or down the road? If you can get the team to commit to finding problems *before* they develop into an event, you will eliminate many future accidents and injuries.

The messages need to be communicated often. Put them up in break rooms, cover them during safety briefs, hang them over urinals, post them in break rooms. Be committed. The words communicate to your team they are important. The more you share it the more people will believe it, and start to make better decisions about their personal safety and teams.

We also started a safety council made up of supervisors from each of the six states. This is an important step because you can't do it alone. You must have the help from your more passionate team members. The safety council was charged and empowered to create its own safety manual (this is only necessary if the corporate manual doesn't cover your duties); to review all our safety rules and best practices to ensure they were correct; to come up with ideas to protect team members; to be advocates for safety throughout the workplace; to be safety leaders for others to emulate; and to conduct an annual assessment to keep a finger on the pulse of performance. All this and other initiatives were put into a business plan so we could communicate this message to the entire department.

"You can't have excellence without great teamwork."

—Lou Holtz

More importantly, I communicated my message every time I shook a team member's hand or gave someone praise for a job well done. I communicated my message when I remembered a spouse's name or engaged a team member about the big football game coming up on Sunday night. I communicated my message of love, trust, commitment, and belief when I offered a team member a heartfelt birthday wish or condolences for the loss of a loved one. When team members know that I genuinely like them and genuinely care about them, if I ever had to coach or correct them regarding something they were doing wrong and/or unsafely, they would take it well because they would know it was coming from a place of love and respect.

As a team leader seeking to create this type of team culture, you must be willing to aggressively do the following. I want to give a shout-out here to my friend and one of the best safety reps I've ever known, Walt Pollard. Many of the following ideas were his passions.

1. Be driven from within. You can read about it and you can talk about it, but you must make a personal commitment to make it happen. Engage people on their strengths. (This idea comes from *Becoming a Person of Influence* by John C. Maxwell, one of my favorite authors on the topic of leadership.)

2. When you engage your team members on their strengths, they recognize there is something they can do well and take pride in themselves because you noticed. That creates the kind of energy that empowers team members to take initiative and to aspire to become leaders of safety and change. Great things happen when people know that you believe and trust them to make a difference in working toward the goal.

3. Catch problems before they hurt a team member. Each team member must be obligated to identify potential problems and communicate them to their leaders and team. This is a huge step in getting to the next level of safety performance. Through my study of human performance and root cause investigations, I'm convinced that nothing just *happens*. There are always signs, smells, noises, something that's not right, or those gut-feeling situations. The problem is that no one takes ownership, and no one feels obligated to investigate and find out if it's a problem or an indicator of a future problem. You must make this an expectation for all team members. Don't be the one who was too busy to investigate a situation that could have saved a person's life.

4. Sweat the small stuff. Often, the small stuff is causing the problems. When team members are injured doing low-hazard, routine work, this is a sign of complacency. Routine work is when people's attention is at its lowest because they've done it a thousand times—then one day it bites them.

5. Only accept perfection. As a safety leader, you must expect perfection from yourself and from everyone else on your team. Even though we're humans and can't ever be perfect on our own, as a team that believes in going the extra mile for each other, we can.

6. Notice when your team members are doing things right. (This idea was introduced to me by Kenneth H. Blanchard and Spencer Johnson in their best-selling book, *The One Minute Manager*, which was first published in 1982.) When you find a team member doing something right, praise them, make a big deal about it. Not a phony big deal but a genuine big deal. It's important that they know that you appreciate and value them.

7. Be a vocal advocate for safety. You cannot sit back in silence during safety meetings or any other time when safety topics are discussed. Don't allow your team to not have comments on the safety topic

discussed that day—go around the room and ask everyone what they think. The more you do this, the team will come to know that you value their comments, and they will become more engaged. Some will even want to lead new initiatives.

8. Be aware of the body language of your team members during safety meetings or safety-related discussions. Body language and facial expressions speak loudly regardless of what is being verbalized. Set the expectations for people to be attentive: play games surrounding safety topics, assign different people to present topics, and allow them to be creative and fun.

When you embrace these principles as a safety leader, you are committing yourself to taking concrete actions to meet the needs of others. When you give with no strings attached, you are making a better *you* by being a servant leader. People respond to those who put others' needs first.

The bad news is that your team's culture won't change overnight, because you can't change your team members. The good news is that your team members will change themselves through respect, love, knowledge, encouragement, motivation, belief in themselves, engagement, nurturing, building on their strengths, listening, understanding, and empowerment. Whenever you advocate for a team culture in which we love each other, trust each other, are committed to each other, and believe in each other, people rush to be part of it. What begins with a few leaders is soon emulated across the company.

When I was supervisor at a nuclear plant, I took over a group of twenty-five mechanics that were considered a tough bunch; they were the most opinionated guys in the whole plant. I was asked, "Bob, how are you going to get these guys motivated?" I was thinking in the back of my head, *With love, trust, commitment, and belief.* I didn't dare say it for fear I'd get laughed out of the building.

The first year, our performance started improving because I figured out that these great folks wanted to be respected and wanted to have their ideas and thoughts listened to and acted upon. This was my first bridge; I began to get to know these guys better—their families, their hobbies, and their passions. We created a list of things they wanted to address. We posted the list in the break room and assigned teams to work on each item. By year's end we had resolved half the list. During that same time, I wove in my expectation on how we needed to respect and treat each other, but I lead the charge by loving these guys. By year two, we were really ironing things out. Next thing you know, we achieved the best safety record in the plant. "How did you do that, Bob?" I was asked. Just how

I always do it: by creating an encouraging team culture based on love, trust, commitment, and belief.

I repeated this same model when I became a plant manager in Goldsboro, North Carolina, but I added to the model the step of spending my initial time with the team of leaders who reported to me, and then the supervisors, in order to build a collaborative, respecting team among leaders first. This got me the buy-in I needed to take this message to the rest of the plant team. I also started asking questions of the team periodically. I called it "How to Engage People."

HOW TO ENGAGE PEOPLE

Communicate:

- your leadership style
- what's important to you/your motives
- what you want/need from your team
- what the team can expect from you
- what culture you want
- your vision
- your plan to get there, a starting point
- how the team needs to work together in order to achieve the goals
- your strengths and weakness

These questions really get to the heart of the matter. Getting the team to answer questions on their leadership style, letting them know what is needed from them and what they can expect from their leader is powerful. Pick the ones you want to use, or share them all over time. This exercise really brings teams closer together.

When I became the general manager responsible for leading five power plants, traveling maintenance, and a project-management team, I did the same thing but added showing some videos during the leadership-team and plant-team sessions. The video I used was titled "Do Right" by Lou Holtz. That video really highlights the love, trust, commitment, and belief message better than I could ever present because it is Lou's message.

Before the video starts, I ask the team to write down the messages they like in the video as it plays. Once it's over, I go around the room and ask each person to share what they liked. This is huge. When folks start sharing their thoughts, their emotions are stirred and their teammates see another side of them. This starts setting the groundwork for change. Then I share my expectation on how we need to treat each other, how we need to work together, and how I will not tolerate anyone mistreating another team member.

ATTRIBUTES OF A GREAT TEAM

- Treat each other as customers.

- Everyone is treated with dignity and respect.

- Provide feedback and coaching.

- Everyone feels valued.

- Communication is open and honest.

- Help resolve issues and concerns.

- Everyone's opinion is valued.

- Seek win-win resolutions to conflict.

- There is respect for each others' processes.

- Use language that does not demean others.

By the end of that session, change is on its way. These messages represent the culture that every human being wants to work in and be a part of. You'll have the majority of the team ready to give it a try.

Fast forward to taking over as general manager of Fleet Services, and I did everything that I've shared here with a large, spread-out team. I made it a top priority to personally visit every one of the fifty-eight locations across six states that were my responsibility. Of course, I was eager to personally let each of my leaders know exactly what I thought of him or her. (I already like you, I already respect you, I already trust you.) Outside of the inevitable safety meetings that I conducted at these locations to begin the process of changing the team culture, I was also looking for those moments where I could set an example—to put the messages I was constantly touting into action.

"See something, say something," is a phrase that's getting a lot of attention around the world these days. In the power industry or any other, caring enough about your fellow employees to speak up about a problem or a situation that might put someone at risk is vital to preventing on-the-job accidents and injuries. As mentioned before, the goal is to get the team engaged in finding potential problems before they injure a teammate. We started ten-minute sessions in the morning where everyone walked around, looking for current and potential problems. The teams did a great job identifying and mitigating those problems, thus avoiding many future injuries. Through my nearly three decades of service to the energy industry, I have been part of far too many investigations into accidents and injuries. In my experience, if I went back far enough in my investigation—a week, a month, six months, a year, two years—I could pinpoint some early indicator or root cause that directly led to each incident. Someone saw something but didn't report it. Because they "didn't want to get involved," the problem slowly developed to the point of the catastrophic failure.

But things happen, right?

Not on my watch.

During a routine safety visit to one of the garages where we were hosting a leadership session (we always had the visiting leaders perform a safety evaluation on the host garage as a way of putting another set of eyes on the building), I saw a gas cylinder lying on the floor under a table with nothing preventing it from rolling. Based on the amount of dust on the cylinder, I knew it had been there a long time. The situation really accentuated my theory on potential, so I wrote it up.

"Oh, come on, Bob. It's been there a long time."

"Aren't you nitpicking?" someone else asked me.

I contend that I was not nitpicking. "Look at this thing," I insisted. "Does anyone see the potential danger?"

So the safety leaders and supervisors stood there looking at the cylinder, shaking their heads, insisting they didn't see the potential danger. Finally, someone in the back spoke up and said, "It could roll."

There it was. Even after that one brave soul pointed out the correct answer, several members of the group kept insisting, "But it's been there for years."

I told them I understood that it had been there for years but asked the question, "What's keeping it from rolling?" Nothing was keeping it from rolling, so it had the potential to roll. It had the potential to roll and hit someone. It had the potential to roll and cause someone to trip and fall. It had the potential to roll to a place where it could be struck by a truck pulling into the garage and cause damage. It had the potential to roll! I understood exactly what could happen if someone backed a truck up against that table, jarred that cylinder, and caused it to roll. Despite all the defensiveness from the supervisors and safety leaders around me, I also knew that choking that cylinder was an easy fix that would probably take less than a minute to remedy. They knew it, too.

The bottom line: the current culture had accepted potential hazards for so long that they were blind to them. This is why we would do these assessments with team members from different locations. Add a fresh set of eyes on situations. The same would be true when we went to the other leaders locations. They would find things that team had become blinded to. These type of assessments are a great tool to promote continuous improvement. When you care enough about your fellow team members, you speak up when you see a potential problem so it can be fixed before someone gets injured. As a leader, it is also your responsibility to listen to your team members when they spot a potential problem and to take steps to resolve it.

While walking through the parking lot during that same inspection, we found a piece of rebar sticking about three feet out of the ground. It had been left by the contractors who had installed the parking curbs, which were made out of railroad ties. It was clear that this rebar had been there for years. It's amazing how we can become blind to potential hazards we see every day. The reason this rebar concerned me was that it was near where people had to climb up and down heavy equipment in order to operate it. During winter or raining conditions when the ground and those railroad ties became slippery, someone could lose their balance, fall, and get impaled by this rebar, resulting in a serious injury or even death. Again, I questioned the team. Folks hadn't seen it or had forgotten it was there but agreed that it was a potential problem. Both items were taken care of.

GETTING TO THE TRUTH ABOUT INCIDENTS OR EVENTS

"If the story or recounting of an event doesn't match the evidence, keep discussing till it does."

—Bob McCall

Here's another situation I'll never forget. I had a team working a major capital improvements job, putting up new poles and power lines in the rural part of a state. The team had cara-vanned to the site that morning, and at the end of its workday, the team was caravanning home. The lead truck made a left turn off a two-lane rural road onto a four-lane highway that would take them back to the shop. The other three trucks followed, all making that left turn at the light. The first three trucks roll down to the next light and stop. The fourth truck came barreling up the highway at fifty-five miles per hour and hit the back of the third truck so hard that it was forced into the second truck, totaling all three trucks. These were bucket trucks worth over $500k each.

The next day, I spent time talking with the supervisor of the team members who were involved in the accident in order to figure out exactly what happened and to determine the root cause. What follows is the story the supervisor got from the driver of the fourth truck, the one who set off the chain reaction:

> When I made the turn, I was looking over at the gas company crew installing some gas lines, and I just happened to notice, you know, because you've taught us so much about safety, that the crew didn't have any trench guards there where they were digging. So when I drove by, I was looking at that, thinking how dangerous it was for those men to be in that trench without the protection of those trench guards. The next thing I knew, I was crashing into the back of the truck.

Really? In other words, the company taught this team member so much about spotting unsafe working situations that his crashing into the back of one of our trucks was actually the company's fault? The driver was so intrigued by another company's unsafe working conditions, so concerned about those people, that he forgot to be concerned about his own team members? The team could tell me that story all day long, but I wasn't buying it.

Over the next few days, I kept hearing about what a great guy the driver of the runaway truck was, what a great worker he was, how he really didn't mean to cause so much damage. "He's one of our best employees." I heard that about a hundred times, and it was all true—he was all that they said he was. He was a great guy, and I loved him and his family as I loved them all. This accident scared us because it could have resulted in some fatalities, but we had to get to the root cause so that this would never happen again. It was uncomfortable for everyone, but not as uncomfortable as it could have been if we lost brothers in that event. The men still functioning in that old team culture were demonstrating the same protectiveness they'd used for years before I arrived. They believed that if they kept repeating the same rendition of the story, I'd eventually give up and let it ride.

This situation led to a principle I always had in place from root cause investigation. "If the story doesn't match the evidence, then we must continue to talk until it does." We experienced protectiveness from supervisors not wanting to see their team members get in trouble, so they would accept any story the members would tell. We had to put a stop to this practice. We were never getting to the real root cause, because we were chasing something that did not happen. We were not learning from our mistakes; we were putting measures in place that had no effect on future accidents because we were trying to fix something that didn't happen. Imagine if we were to let it go and then down the road the same thing happens again, but this time, someone dies. How would we face the families knowing that we hadn't done all we could to prevent this when it happened the last time? How could we live with that guilt?

I had to be determined to get to the truth because I couldn't change the team culture to one focused on love, trust, commitment, and belief *and* fix the safety problem—clearly there was a safety problem that needed to be addressed—if I didn't know the truth. I didn't back off. Eventually, we discovered that the root cause of the accident was that the driver of truck number four was dealing with fatigue behind the wheel. He'd been called in to work in the wee hours of the morning and hadn't gotten the proper rest. Then the worker, along with the rest of the crew, had eaten a heavy lunch, and that was working on him. In the old culture, the men working those crews would never admit being tired for fear of being looked at "as not being able to hold up his end of the job" and likely being teased about it by the team members. From a cultural standpoint, I knew it was important to start dispelling the "he-man" myths right away.

I know just how easy it is to get caught up in these myths because I came from a workplace culture that did just that. Let me tell on myself a little bit here. I remember, early in my career as a piping engineer working at a construction site in Michigan called Belle River, I was reviewing installed pipe with the general foreman. This guy had over thirty years of experience, so everyone really looked up to him. He had picked up a habit of jumping across the pipes, and that practice became an unwritten standard. If you couldn't jump the pipes, you couldn't keep up. I was scared of heights, but more importantly, I was scared of not measuring up to what I thought was the expectation.

Then one day I almost fell. The general foreman asked, "Are you okay, Bob? You know we don't have to jump the pipes; we can walk around."

"We can walk around?" I questioned. "I thought this was the only way. I was scared to ask if there was another way."

He apologized and said, "I should have asked you if you were uncomfortable, but when I looked behind me, you were always there."

I replied, "I was making the jumps—scared to death each time I did one—but didn't want you to think I couldn't keep up."

This example of miscommunication is what happens every day at work sites. This is why I press for the truth and why I stress a culture of love, trust, commitment, and belief. My goal is to eliminate the unwritten pressures and miscommunications that can result in injuries or even deaths on work sites.

As the leader, I didn't get to the truth by calling the driver (or anyone protecting him) a liar. I didn't start cussing and being mad, because I knew they would not respond with malicious behavior. Nevertheless, I knew that I had to get to the truth and follow up by fixing the problem because the next time this crewman got tired and fell asleep behind the wheel of a half-million-dollar truck, he or someone else could be seriously injured or even killed.

"Did any of you realize he hadn't gotten the proper rest and was tired?" I asked the other team members.

"Yes, he mentioned it … several times."

"Was his performance suffering?"

"Maybe a little," they replied.

We started enforcing the policy on how many hours straight a crewman was allowed to work without sleep. We reviewed the proper way to report a problem a crew member discovers on the job site, such as a worker who is not able to complete the task properly and safely. We went over what crewmen could say to another worker in a similar situation. The trucks weren't fixable, but my experience told me that the team culture was.

There have been countless times over my many years in the energy industry when injuries and accidents have occurred because workers failed to recognize their individual limitations. As we age, our bodies can't always do what they did when we were young.

I remember one teammate at one of my locations who injured himself grabbing a reel of Triplex. When he was young, he could pick up a reel, which probably weighed eighty pounds, and toss it around like a ragdoll. Now he was fifty-nine years old, so when he reached around and grabbed the reel of Triplex, he pulled his back. It took a sprained back and time off work for him to realize he couldn't do everything the way he had for the last thirty years. This is one of the hardest things for men: to recognize we're not as young as we once were. Let me tell on myself with a funny story where I refused to recognize my own limitations.

When my family and I lived in Clayton, North Carolina, we owned a home with a two-story entryway. Above the door, there were windows that let the natural light flood in. And it just so happened that right under the top window was a ledge.

My wife, Benita, and I decided that ledge would be a great place to put some Christmas decoration that could be seen from the outside. The ledge was about two-and-a-half feet wide and was already equipped with power outlets.

Being the highly intelligent and observant man that I am, I noticed that one of the steps up to the second floor was just about level with the ledge. I walked up the steps to check it out. Sure enough, there was no doubt in my mind that if I contorted my body just a little, I could stretch one leg out and hoist myself onto that ledge, even with a box of Christmas decoration in my arms, to avoid having to go all the way to the garage to get the extension ladder.

Just as I was about to put my theory to the test, I hear from below me, "What do you think you're doing?" I didn't have to answer, because she already knew. "Go to the garage and get your extension ladder before you get hurt." My wife did not use the term "knucklehead" when she spoke to me, but it was clearly implied in her tone. When I hesitated a moment to prepare my little speech as to why this was such a good idea, she let loose with, "Get your stupid self down from there right now and go get that ladder!" (My wife didn't actually say, "stupid self," but again, I'm pretty sure it was implied.) "You teach and expect your team to do the right thing, and look at you," she added.

I stomped off to the garage feeling highly offended at being talked to as if I were a small child being scolded by his mother. *My own wife thinks I'm too old and feeble to make that small leap from the step to that ledge! Has she forgotten that I am a highly respected and beloved leader of high-performing teams at work?*

Work. There was that. There were a number of possible variables in this situation, but one thing was for sure: if I'd fallen and injured myself, I'd have never lived it down at work.

"Why isn't Bob at work today?" someone would eventually ask.

"Didn't you hear? He fell off a ledge at his house. He sprained his back and broke his wrist and won't be in for a week, maybe more."

"What happened? Didn't he secure his ladder properly?"

"What ladder?" my concerned coworker would reply, followed by uproarious laughter. My body may have healed, but my ego and reputation as a leader would never fully recover.

Here's the bottom line: my wife cared enough about me to speak up and say something when she saw a situation that could result in my injury, or worse, my demise. (I like to think she learned that from me.) My wife *expected* more from me.

Don't be like me. We don't need he-men reporting to work every day. I wanted men (and women) who were able to recognize their individual limitations and ask for help when they needed it. And I wanted teammates who would step up and help when they were asked. To get both required a change in the team culture. Be the leader who let's the team know you don't want them hurt and your willing to challenge them to get help. There's no shame to the game of needing help. We all do and will if we work long enough.

STEP UP AND TAKE ACTION

Leaders step up. Leaders take action. Leaders identify the potential sources of accidents and injuries and do whatever they can to eliminate them.

"Listen up, team. Amanda says there's a hole in the field. Let's all go take a look."

As a leader, you point out the hole so everyone on the team can avoid it. You grab a couple of those safety cones you saw in the parking lot on your way in and use them to mark both sides of the hole. You call and leave a message at the league office regarding the hole and the potential of someone stepping in it and falling. And even though you know your spouse is taking the roast out of the oven right about now, you stick around a few minutes after practice to make sure the coach of the next team scheduled to practice knows about the hole. Then you follow up with a call to the league office in the morning.

Your team members may know all the safety rules by heart, they may have great skills to do their jobs, they may have opened their eyes again to potential hazards, and you may be making strides in getting every team member to embrace the new culture that will allow them to achieve a high level of performance, but if they don't have the proper tools and equipment, and if their work environment isn't safe, accidents and injuries are going to continue to happen.

On my initial journey to visit all fifty-eight facilities I was in charge of at Fleet Services, I remember going to both small and large garages. Some of those facilities were dark and dingy and had grease and spiderwebs all over the walls, air conditioners that didn't work, many major tools that were old and outdated, paint peeling off walls, and more. In most cases, due to these conditions, there were accidents just waiting to happen.

"How long has it been since this piece of equipment worked?" I asked.

The men answered with shrugs, and a few mumbled I-don't-knows. "Did anyone report that it needed to be repaired?" I pressed.

I waited. Finally, one of the men spoke up. "I think Ed reported it, but no one showed up to fix it. Since *they* weren't interested in fixing that, we just figured ..."

"Ed? Which one of you is Ed?"

"Oh, Ed hasn't worked here for a couple of years."

Good for Ed. I wouldn't want to report to work every day to a place like this, either. I pulled out my pen and positioned it over the paper on my clipboard. "Tell me, what do you gentlemen need?"

They were shy at first, but because in earlier messages they knew I loved, respected, and appreciated them, it was easy to get them talking, and my paper quickly filled up. We walked through the facility again, with me making notes of what exactly needed to be repaired and what was junk that needed to be removed. I made detailed notes on all the structural repairs and improvements that were needed. I checked out the men's personal tools and safety equipment and made notes on what was still in good working order, what was missing, and what had to be upgraded. By the end of my visit, the technicians knew that I cared enough about their safety—about getting them home to their families every night—to listen to their needs. I was about to prove to them just how much I cared.

When I returned to my office, I put together a plan involving expanding our tools and equipment team. I asked one of my directors to lead the team, so he got representatives from each region, and together they developed a charter and started to measure all the garages. They developed a standard, communicated it to the department, and prioritized it as we secured more funding than in the past. Soon folks started receiving the new tools and equipment that was being replaced and/or upgraded. The team made sure that all the potential safety hazards were identified and eliminated. In essence, the leadership team and I made sure the hole was filled.

The technicians knew we cared, and performance improved. We started a team with the responsibility of reviewing all our garages, making assessments, prioritizing, and then providing recommendations on which garages to repair. Garages were painted, floors cleaned, break rooms cleaned and painted, air conditioning units repaired, new lighting installed, and walls washed. Performance improved because we cared enough to do something.

During my visit to the first site, I could have taken the team out for a nice dinner, gotten to know them a little, and given my pitch about creating an encouraging team culture based on love, trust, commitment, and belief. Or maybe I could have done what a number of other safety leaders do in our industry: slapped these hard-working crewmen with another big stack of new safety rules to learn.

But instead, I chose to lead, have a vision, get the leadership team involved, engage the people, ask for help, empower the team, support them, reward them, and praise them. If I hadn't stepped up, if I hadn't taken action, all my words and good intentions wouldn't have meant a thing. Now when we go to dinner, it's meaningful.

Maybe you're thinking that in your current position as a leader, you don't have the authority to do everything I did to improve the working conditions of the garages. Whatever your job description, you have the power to step up, speak up, and follow up. As a leader, it's your responsibility to set the example company wide. Before long, other employees will be stepping up, speaking up, and following up.

I shudder to think about how many argon cylinders are left lying around unchoked because someone didn't want to be accused of being a nitpicker, how much rebar is sticking up out of the ground, how many spills are walked around because someone had better things to worry about, or how many holes go unfilled because someone couldn't wait to get home to a hot dinner.

Remember: you're a leader, and you *can* make a difference!

INDIVIDUAL EXPECTATIONS

CHAPTER 3: INDIVIDUAL EXPECTATIONS

*"You don't strengthen the weak
by weakening the strong."*

—Lou Holtz

Pay attention because the next sentence is vitally important to leaders who are committed to changing the team culture in their organization: you must change individual expectations to match the vision of the culture you want. This will produce high-performing behaviors within team players, but it's only through working together with your fellow employees that your team can achieve the goal of ZERO first aid cases, recordable injuries, lost-time accidents, fatalities, and controllable vehicle accidents and incidents. If you show enough confidence, if you have enough belief, if you're willing to take the lead—you can get other people to believe.

> *You must change individual expectations to match the vision of the culture you want.*
>
> *"You can't have excellence without great teamwork."*
>
> —Lou Holtz

I like to use sports analogies to explain. If you want to be a starter on any sports team, you must meet the expectation needed to play that position at the highest level. The coach doesn't lower the expectations for the positions to meet your skill level. The coach knows that he needs the best players playing if the team is going to win. That's why I love the Lou Holtz quote, "You don't strengthen the weak by weakening the strong." In all his years of coaching and winning divisional and national championships, he knew the caliber of athlete that needed to be on the field. So do you in the working world. Expectations for your team to demonstrate winning behaviors will develop winners and stir up the winners you already have on the team. The expectation for your team to model champion behaviors will do the same—create champions and stir up the ones you have. Why do you want to stir up the ones in the group? Because they will be your initial "starters." They will be your volunteers to lead projects, lead improvement teams, be safety chairpersons, and be strong advocates for the culture change. Once they see what you need to make the team successful and know those skills match what they have inside themselves, they're going to want to be a part of this movement. Let me give you the two lists of winners and champions. I made up the winner behavior list, but the list of champion behaviors comes from Lee Labrada, champion bodybuilder from the 1980s.

These are winner behaviors:

- being a good spouse and good parent

- giving back to the community

- being the best person that you can be

- treating everyone with respect

- helping each other

- doing your part to help build a better team

- going the extra mile for team members

These are the champion behaviors:

- focuses on goals

- takes action

- does what needs to be done

- moves with enthusiasm

- overcomes obstacles

- likes himself or herself

- does it now

- holds himself or herself accountable

Aren't these great? Imagine if you had a team that came to work every day modeling these behaviors. There would be no challenges this team couldn't overcome. Remember, you must model these behaviors if you want the team to.

"Come to work every day ready to give your best (200 percent)—100 percent for you and 100 percent for the team."

—Bob McCall, Inspire High Performance

Another tool that is helpful when shaping expectations is called "The Partnership." I got the idea years ago from Allstate insurance while studying diversity and inclusion. The Allstate version reads, "… a set of mutual expectations between the company and employees. The Partnership describes what employees can expect from Allstate as an employer and what, in turn, the company expects from employees."[2] I liked the concept but customized it to match the needs of my industry. I suggest you do the same for your industry. If you can't think of any words, use these to get started.

---

2   "Allstate Culture," Allstate, https://www.allstate.com/careers/culture.aspx.

I liked the phrase "Partnership" because it takes a partnership to make this happen. You and the team both have to be willing to work together for the safety of everyone.

THE PARTNERSHIP

What I Expect from You (Your Team):

- to work in a safe manner with equipment and personnel
- to be the best on the job
- to take the time to do the job right the first time
- to suggest ideas that improve and enhance the work process and work environment
- to challenge yourself to be better at your job
- to embrace company goals and requirements
- to treat each other with dignity and respect
- to have a positive attitude

What You Should Expect from Me:

- a workplace that is committed to safety, that supports and rewards good work
- a workplace that is committed to excellence
- a workplace that is considerate of ideas
- a workplace that encourages team development
- a workplace that has high standards
- a workplace that embraces diversity principles
- a workplace that is transparent

I want you to have this group of expectations that also help move the team to another level. Once again, my friend Walt Pollard shared some expectations that helped us connect and get to the next level. I want to give you the ones that resonate in people. I'll bold the words that have extreme significance. The goal is to use these to help you shape your expectations for the person that best serves your industry.

1. Every employee must understand that **working without an accident or injury is expected.**

2. Team members must **respect each other** and care enough about their fellow team members and themselves to be **willing** to personally **go the extra mile** for them. Every team member must be held accountable for **speaking up** in meetings and **respectfully** challenging others when questionable behaviors are observed.

3. Team members must **trust** the team and the company.

4. Team members must be **committed** to the team, the vision, and the mission of the company. They must **actively** support safety rules, initiatives, policies, and procedures and must come to work every day ready to give their best. They must **ask** for assistance when they need it.

5. Team members must care enough about their fellow employees to speak up when they **think** something isn't right. Team members are **obligated** to identify **potential** problems and **communicate** them to their safety leaders and their team.

6. Team members must be able to **accept** constructive criticism as an indication that others **care about their well-being**.

7. Team members must make a **personal** commitment to change the team culture.

8. Team members must be vocal **advocates** for safety. They must ask questions if they are not sure of a rule or process.

I love number five. The word "obligated" is huge. Ask your team what this word means to them. This is one you want to make an expectation. When the team or crew becomes obligated to each other, sold on finding potential and existing problems, and makes it part of their team/crew culture. When new members join the crew, the crew welcomes the new team member and let's them know they are now part of our work family. We look out for each other, we go the extra mile for each other, we care and respect each other. We will nurture you so you learn. Your word means something today. We extend love, trust, commitment and belief to you. This is the way a new person should be welcomed, you want all your crews to show this level of leadership. When they do, you're on your way to "ZERO" and to leaving a legacy for the future.

Performance evaluations are another tool you can use to set expectations. Many of you may already have one that the company uses, but I urge you to at least review some of the words we used to see if they get to the behaviors you want better than your current evaluation form. Here are the core skills we use in the form of an evaluation. Some are specific of expectations applicable to those working in the power industry but that can be used for any industry, or you can amend them to fit your industry. The goal is to use these in a performance evaluation, so these expectations are being discussed twice a year. It's the best way to keep the message out there—reinforce the expectations and monitor the team performance and improvement. It also gives you a great opportunity to coach if team members are not performing up to expectations. This will make it sustainable.

CORE SKILLS THAT CHANGE AND IMPROVE CULTURE

Craftsmanship

- consistently performs high-quality work; performs to the correct standards with no or minimal rework required

- completes all necessary documentation accurately and on time

- provides immediate, factual, and complete information to supervisors, fellow employees, and customers

- demonstrates proficiency in the designated tasks within the defined time frames

- adheres to company policies and procedures

Interpersonal Skills

- demonstrates the goal of listening and positively responding to others by acknowledging them, using positive word choices, not interrupting others, and using positive tone of voice and body language

- communicates options and alternative solutions rather than only discussing the problems

- communicates clearly and respectfully with customers, and does so proactively whenever possible

- actively engages and participates in meetings

- provides timely and constructive feedback, guidance, and instruction to others

- does not engage in disrespectful or disruptive behavior through word choice, tone, or action

Problem Solving

- solves problems independently when appropriate
- adjusts work plans where appropriate and according to changing conditions
- offers suggestions for continuous business improvement
- identifies personal skill or knowledge gaps and addresses them appropriately
- asks questions, including asking for assistance when needed

Productivity

- makes efficient use of time in completing tasks, without compromising safety and quality while prioritizing work appropriately
- minimizes unproductive time, such as not wasting time at meetings, when traveling, or near end of the day
- meets required due dates, deadlines, and commitments
- effectively and efficiently uses and reuses resources and materials as appropriate
- responds positively to change by adopting, supporting, and sustaining it
- consistently arrives at work on time and is physically and mentally prepared

- cultivates diversity and inclusion by making supportive statements and actively engaging in related initiatives and events

- suggests ideas that will streamline tasks and processes while not compromising safety and quality of work

- responds in a timely manner to emergent work needs, both on duty and after hours

Safety

- complies with the health and safety manual and all safety-related policies

- verifies that pretrip and post-trip inspections are performed correctly and as required

- actively looks for, identifies, and mitigates hazards

- demonstrates actively caring by intervening when appropriate to keep fellow employees safe, reporting and sharing close calls, and entering events into a corrective-action program

- demonstrates safety as a value by leading "take tens" and prejob/job planning briefings and participating in safety councils and safety programs

- routinely inspects appropriate dates and condition of tools and equipment and addresses issues as required

- maintains a safe and orderly work environment including vehicle, equipment, job site, and workspace

- identifies and escalates ideas for new tools, processes, procedures, and equipment that improve safety
- utilizes three-point communication, peer checking, self-checking, and other human-performance tools

Teamwork

- assists others when own work is complete
- coordinates work with other departments and classifications as appropriate
- collaborates and compromises to achieve the best results for the team
- successfully passes on best practices and learned job skills and knowledge to others by providing instruction, assistance, and coaching
- participates in committees and on special projects as assigned
- reconciles differences of opinion by speaking assertively with facts and directing the resolution toward the greater good of the organization

The last tool is getting your team to believe in themselves because when they do, they'll set higher expectations for themselves. You get them to believe in themselves by emphasizing their strengths and giving them opportunities to serve on teams. Stop letting people sit on the sidelines and punt problems at you. Get them involved. Also, don't put the hardheads on the teams. Put your best people on the teams—the ones who model the behaviors of winners and champions. This is the way you get energy going. Get the team involved with your department's safety initiatives—allow strong team members to lead teams and be major players. Give them the expectations, and be thinkers and action takers. Empower them, monitor their progress, and get ready to praise them when they hit home runs.

Before long, the team culture will start taking on a life of its own. As a leader, that's exactly what you want. That's how you create a legacy of safety performance that will last long after you've moved on.

Creating an encouraging team culture focused on love, trust, commitment, and belief may begin with leadership—your leadership—but will only improve your team's safety performance when it permeates the attitudes of every team member. When you expect every employee to be a safe employee, they will strive everyday to work without an accident or injury. Then it starts to spread throughout the team and company.

BEHAVIORS THAT CANNOT BE TOLERATED BECAUSE THEY DESTROY TEAM PERFORMANCE

CHAPTER 4: BEHAVIORS THAT CANNOT BE TOLERATED BECAUSE THEY DESTROY TEAM PERFORMANCE

This is going to be the most challenging area for implementation because it involves addressing behaviors that may have been allowed for years and have become the norm. It's also personal because some of the people who possess these behaviors can be your best working employees, the guy you started work with, your fishing or hunting buddy, or the guy who is friends with the boss. The measures you take here may cause you to become unpopular. I do strongly encourage you to move forth—don't let this chapter scare you away from addressing these behaviors. I like the term behaviors. When you put the focus on behaviors, it takes away from this being personal. It's bigger that you and the person who demonstrates the behavior. This is about the success of the team.

Throughout the many years I have studied leadership and human performance, I have gleaned valuable information from many sources and repurposed it to apply to the power industry. I also believe these principles will work for any type of industry or organization. Using all I've learned (and continue to learn), I began to pave a path to higher safety performance using the methods I've presented so far in this book.

Trust me; there was a learning curve. Despite my hands-on successes in pursuing my ZERO vision in my early days as a leader, I'd occasionally hit a roadblock along the way. As I looked around for the reasons why my team's performance wasn't climbing upward as it should, something important finally occurred to me. Certain team members were behaving in ways that inhibited the cultivation of an encouraging team culture focused on love, trust, commitment, and belief. Further investigation, along with a lot of trial and error, quickly revealed that I was on the right track.

There are six behaviors that ruin team performance. Unfortunately, if the people demonstrating these behaviors have sway or influence on others in their groups, studies have shown that the standards of the group as a whole begin a downward trajectory toward those negative behaviors. Therefore, if you allow the teammate exhibiting these behaviors to take over any group, you're not going to be successful in changing your team culture and getting your safety performance to a higher level. As a leader, it's important for you to be able to recognize these six behaviors and to deal with them promptly and effectively. The way to begin to confront these behaviors is to address the person in a way that questions whether or not they are aware of their actions: "Hey Bob, can I speak with you a moment? Are you aware that every time an idea is brought up, you *always* have something negative to say?"

"Bob, are you aware that you always try to speak for the team, instead of stating your own position and letting the rest of the team members express theirs?"

"Bob, are you aware that those jokes you tell or the way you tease the team members hurts their feelings?"

As I go down the list of behaviors, you will quickly begin to recognize people in your life—both work life and personal life—that display these bad behaviors.

Once you point out the bad behaviors in these people, your team begins to realize how these personalities can destroy team performance. But your efforts to neutralize and/or eliminate these bad behaviors should not turn into opportunities to embarrass people or hurt their feelings. After all, the goal is not to get rid of your teammate. The goal is to get rid of your teammate's bad behavior.

Once again, here's the phrase that usually nips these bad behaviors in the bud and how you want to start the conversation: "Are you aware ...?"

BEHAVIORS THAT CANNOT BE TOLERATED

The **complainer** is a person who offers no solutions but just complains.

The **negative attitude** is a person who is always down and always identifying the worst in a situation.

The **bully** is a person who puts everyone else's ideas down, disrespects the team, devalues other people's opinions, and intimidates other team members.

The **teaser** is a person who makes personal attacks through joking, racial comments, or sexist comments and who hurts the feelings of other team members.

The **straight shooter** is a person who knows everyone else's faults but will acknowledge none of his or her own. This type of person can never take it as straight as he or she gives it.

The **self-proclaimed spokesperson** is a person who uses the team to forward his or her own agenda.

THE COMPLAINER

A complainer is the person who complains, but never has a solution to fix it. As a team leader, it's your responsibility to shut down this bad behavior. Here's how:

Joe, are you aware that you are a complainer? When we brought up the new hard-hat policy at the last safety meeting, you stood up and complained. When I asked you if there was something else that you'd seen that we could use instead, you didn't have anything to say. Then, when we started the fire-hose policy, you got up and complained about that, too. When I asked you if you knew of anything that could maybe work better, you had nothing to offer.

Simply present the complainer with the times he or she complained without offering any solutions. Then make it clear to the complaining Joe that he needs to change because his behavior is destroying team performance. That approach keeps it from being considered personal by the person whose behavior you're correcting. It's all about the team's performance, although when you hold people's lives in your hands, it can sometimes feel personal.

THE NEGATIVE ATTITUDE

The negative attitude is always identifying the worst in any situation. It's common to celebrate a successful safety year with a meal. The negative person will comment on what we eat. If the team suggests hamburgers the negative person wants steak. If the team wants steak, the negative person wants hot dogs.

There's always that one person needling with a negative comment, trying to find the worst in everything. That same team member mocked an ice-cream social we put together to celebrate a first quarter without an accident in one division. "Just ice cream," he snipped. "Why can't we get a steak dinner?" For me, any day I can take a break and eat ice cream at work is a great day. But if you allow one person's negative attitude to infect the attitudes of other team members, that person is hurting overall team performance. Don't let that person get away with it.

Post this message for all to see: A bad attitude is like a flat tire. If you don't change it, you'll never go anywhere. Once again, start the conversation off with the question, "Are you aware...." Here's another comment you can make: "Do you realize your actions can destroy the team's performance? You have to stop; as a leader responsible for this team, I must ask you to stop. I can't have you endangering the lives of the team."

THE STRAIGHT SHOOTER

I've taken a lot of flak for including the straight shooter on my list of behaviors that cannot be tolerated. "He's just an honest person telling it like it is, right?"

The person I'm talking about is not the honest person but rather the person who know everyone's faults but acknowledges none of his or her own. They're the tough guys—the people who put others down to make themselves look better. They're the people who can't take it as straight as they give it.

"Why can't anyone do anything right around here?" they lament. "I don't even know why I work here." But as soon as you pull out something they didn't do correctly, they want to fight you.

When I played high school and college football, I wanted tough guys in front of me. But in the workplace, we don't need tough guys. You're tough enough if you come to work every day ready to do a good job and look out for your teammates. You're tough enough if you take care of your family and give back to your community.

I love what Coach Lou Holtz has to say about tough guys. "If you've got to put people down to make yourself feel big, you've got low self-esteem. I don't care if you're seven-foot tall and weigh nine hundred pounds, you've got low self-esteem." That's the straight shooter in a nutshell.

THE BULLY

We all remember the bullies of our youths—the boys (usually) who picked on the smallest and physically weakest kids and took their lunch money and their cool school supplies. Unlike the bullies we knew and were victimized by when we were children and teenagers, bullies in the workplace aren't taking our lunch money. Instead, they are stealing team performance. They do that by putting down other people's ideas. They devalue other people's opinions. They disrespect the team. This is the bully of our modern-day workplace.

When the new hire—say, a twenty-three-year-old who has been on the job less than a year, for example—comes up with an idea, it's the bully who says, "That isn't going to work. We tried that five years ago. How long has he been here? He doesn't know anything. I've been here thirty years, so I know what I'm talking about."

By the way, just because this bully has been getting his way for thirty years through intimidation and by devaluing and disrespecting others doesn't mean he should get away with it any longer. Leadership takes courage, and as a leader who values your teammates and is committed to creating an encouraging new culture, it's your job to shut down bullies. Remember the phrase that pays big dividends in shutting down bad behavior: "Are you aware …?"

THE TEASER

Every company has at least one funny guy (or gal): the practical joker, the comedian. I'm not against using a little laughter to get through the day. I was teased regularly about being a Steelers fan, which was all in good fun. The teasers are often smart-alecks who always have a joke to tell. But when the teaser tells off-color jokes, or womanizing jokes, or racial jokes, he's out of bounds. So is teasing about stature, health issues, or anything to do with someone's family. When the teaser crosses the line into embarrassing other teammates and hurting their feelings, it's time to step up and put a stop to it.

The power industry has been dominated by the tough-guy attitude for decades, but things are changing in all industries, including this one. More and more women are taking on jobs that were once the exclusive domain of men. Diversity is huge. America is changing, and people look different than they used to. All this means is that the talent pool is getting larger. Companies have to be ready to welcome this new group of talent. You can no longer have someone on staff who is against welcoming new Americans.

I'm reminded of a meeting I was facilitating where one of the technicians made a negative comment about us hiring women. Then in another conversation he was angry that his daughter wasn't getting opportunities to advance because of the men dominating that industry. When I heard him make that statement, I reminded him of what he'd said about hiring women. Crazy, right? But that's how some people think. We must have the expectation for men to clean up their act. We can't go around saying inappropriate things to our teammates—no sexual jokes, no jokes about a person's looks, etc.

One teammate I worked with for many years had to undergo a couple of shoulder surgeries. After thirty-seven years as a lineman, working overhead, it is likely that you're going to have problems with your shoulders. One day I overheard one of the young linemen teasing him about not being able to hold up his end of the bargain anymore and not being able to carry his own weight. Wait just a minute; that's not what we say to each other. As a leader, I stepped up. I pointed out to the young man that he didn't know how he was going to age. When people work hard outdoors all of their lives, their bodies are going to break down. It might be a shoulder, a knee, or a back.

As a leader, it's important for me to always step up and speak up when I encounter this type of bad behavior from teammates.

I never stand by and allow a teammate to hurt another's feelings, because it ultimately causes division and hurts team performance. As a leader, if you ever walk by a teaser exhibiting this bad behavior without taking a stand against it, you condone the behavior, so I hope you're prepared to work twice as hard to try to salvage the team's safety performance when it starts to slip. So the next time you encounter a teaser, step up. Show courage. Here's how you start: "Hey, Howard, are you aware that you're a teaser?"

THE SELF-PROCLAIMED SPOKESPERSON

Anyone who has sat through safety meetings knows exactly who the self-proclaimed spokesperson of the group is. When the safety leaders ask for a volunteer, the self-proclaimed spokesperson is on his or her feet, taking full advantage of an opportunity to push his or her own agenda.

"The rest of the folks here don't want to talk, Bob, but I'll tell you," says the self-proclaimed spokesperson. Any phrase similar to that one makes my antenna go up.

The self-proclaimed spokesperson is also skilled at using phrases such as, "The team got together and we decided ..." as a way to push his or her own agenda. As I look around the room, the body language of the other teammates tells me something else entirely. I see people looking at the spokesperson as if they're asking, "When did we ever agree to that?" Sometimes, I even see panic in their eyes.

The self-proclaimed spokesperson requires special handling. This is how I've handled this bad behavior a number of times throughout my career.

"Hold on there, just a minute," I say. "I'm sorry to interrupt you, but I need some clarification on something. Don't sit down ... stay right there."

Then I probe the room. "Betty, do you need this person to speak for you? Or can you speak for yourself as the intelligent woman that you are?"

"I can speak for myself, Bob," replies Betty.

"How about you, Jim?" I continue. "Do you need this person to speak for you? Or can you speak for yourself as the intelligent man that you are?"

Instead of letting the self-proclaimed spokesperson off the hook too easily, I continue around the room asking others. After I've probed the room, I turn to the self-proclaimed spokesperson and say, "I don't think these folks need you to speak for them. In fact, everyone is going to get an opportunity to speak for themselves. So what's your opinion?"

Nine times out of ten, the self-proclaimed spokesperson just sits down without anything more to say. The plan to forward a personal agenda using the team for backup has failed. As a result, I've empowered the other people in the room to get engaged in the process because I've already let them know that I think they are intelligent people and they are valued because I'm giving them an opportunity to speak and share their ideas.

Never let the bad behavior of a self-proclaimed spokesperson take root. As a leader, when you use the go-around-the-room tactic, you encourage an environment of collaboration. Once you get a number of folks willing to talk, be sure to listen to what they have to say, then respond positively to their ideas using phrases such as, "That's a good point," or "I appreciate you bringing that up," or "That's something we need to talk about further," or "Thank you so much," or "Mary just put a big question on the table, so let's discuss it further." The next thing you know, you'll hear others—directors, supervisors, safety leaders—using these same phrases in the meetings they conduct. It's a beautiful thing to watch good behaviors fill the voids created where bad behaviors have been shut down.

These unacceptable behaviors surround or influence most injuries. I'm reminded of two stories I want to share that I hope will encourage you.

At one of my centers, there was a guy who had been there many years. I loved him like I loved all my team members. He had a little smart-alecky way about him. It was subtle, but it was always there—getting in the last word in discussions, making jokes about some rules or direction from the top, and not supporting decisions. Mind you, when everybody had the chance to share their opinions, he didn't. He was also the guy talking about the wrong things at the job site, causing team members to be distracted.

I warned him early on that he needed to be careful with his attitude because folks could take it as him being a smart butt. Well, during a storm—when our workers take on the role of team leaders to guide the contractors who support us—he neglected to do his role properly and put one of our contractors in danger. A close call almost seriously injured the contractor who trusted that we had done our job well. During the root cause investigation, it was discovered that the employee didn't do what he was supposed to do. After storms and power lines are down, it's important that we, the host utility, ensure lines are de-energized and grounded before our contractors work in those areas. This was not done, putting a person's life in danger. We had to let the employee go.

His team was very angry at me for doing this. They were mad for about three months, but then one of the team members came to me and said, "We didn't realize how much that person was tearing the team apart, how he was always stirring up crap all the time. We have become much closer since he has been gone." This is why my conviction is so strong in this area.

Another situation occurred at a center where a supervisor didn't like the direction the company was headed regarding its use of work packages (planning processes to assist us in doing our work). This supervisor, who had a straight-shooter, tough-guy personality, hated the idea of planned work packages, and his behavior was not addressed. One day while on a job, he totally ignored a work package that contained four warnings that needed to be heeded in order to perform the job safely. But this supervisor didn't bother to even open the package. He had that "I've-been-doing-this-job-for-years-and-don't-need-no-work-package-to-tell-me-how-to-do-my-job" attitude. So he sent his apprentice into the very area the work package warned about, resulting in his partner sustaining a career-ending injury that almost ended his life. After the fact, the supervisor had to deal with the guilt over the fact that it was his hard-headed attitude that caused a team member's career to be over.

You must take these examples to heart and be encouraged to start dealing with these behaviors. People's lives may depend on you taking action.

Just to recap—in order to get to a higher level of safety performance, you, as a leader, need the right leadership skills and an all-encompassing but attainable vision such as ZERO first aid cases, recordable injuries, lost-time accidents, fatalities, and controllable vehicle accidents and incidents. You need to create an encouraging team culture focused on love, trust, commitment, and belief and advance that culture by letting team members know exactly what you expect from them. As your new culture begins to evolve organically, you protect it by neutralizing or eliminating those who knowingly or unknowingly sabotage the vision and the new culture with their bad behaviors. As the new team culture takes root, members of your team will get engaged. The team's level of respect and appreciation grows toward one another, people start loving to come to work and follow the existing safety rules at a higher level (they start finding potential problems before they cause an event), and everybody buys into improving the company's overall safety performance—not for the numbers but because they love each other and want to protect each other. No new safety rules required!

As a leader, you set the example. However, it's everyone's responsibility to help create and sustain a culture where every member of the team can realize his or her top potential every single day. It's everyone's responsibility to cherish the culture and promote it and sustain it. It's your responsibility to get rid of those team members who don't measure up.

Now there's just one last thing you need to do to maintain your team's high level of safety performance. I call it "hiring winners."

HIRING WINNERS WITH CHAMPION BEHAVIORS

CHAPTER 5: HIRING WINNERS WITH CHAMPION BEHAVIORS

"A champion is someone you become through a process of self-improvement, sacrifice, service, and yes, the attainment of goals normally out of the reach of all except those willing to pay the price."

—Lee Labrada, champion bodybuilder

During my long career working in the power industry, I served in many roles. Each time I was given the opportunity to take on a new challenge, I inherited a new team—a group of men and women of varying experiences and backgrounds—that I was responsible to lead. From the day my dear friend was carried out of the Hope Creek Nuclear Generating Station following an industrial accident, I knew the most important responsibility I have had has been ensuring the safety of my entire team. I have the responsibility to work safely so that I make it home to my wife and children every night. I have the responsibility to have the backs of my brothers and sisters so they make it home to their families every night. I have the responsibility to step up, speak up, and follow up when I see problems that could result in accidents and injuries. Despite what it said on my job description during any phase of my career, being a safety leader never stopped being a top priority for me.

With every new team I inherited as I progressed through my thirty-plus-year career, I moved through the steps I've outlined in this book in order to change the culture and take the team to a higher level of safety performance. It worked every time I tried it! No exceptions. I have the statistics to prove it. When your division starts reporting fewer first aid cases, fewer recordable injuries, fewer lost-time accidents, fewer fatalities, and fewer controllable vehicle accidents and incidents, you know you are on the right track to achieving the vision of ZERO in all those categories. And when you see that begin to happen, you know you have surrounded yourself with winners—team members who choose to perform at their highest level every day.

Every new group you inherit to lead will likely already consist of a large percentage of winners. Many may just be waiting for the right kind of leadership that will encourage them to excel—to be the best they can be. As you start to nurture an encouraging team culture within your organization, your teammates will begin to step up their game just to be part of the amazing, organic phenomenon going on at work. Sure, you'll have your share of those who exhibit bad behaviors—the complainers, the negative attitudes, the bullies, the teasers, the straight shooters, and the self-proclaimed spokespeople—that are welcome to make the journey if they decide to change their beliefs, their attitude, their behavior and performance. If not, show them the door. You can not allow those behaviors to continue, or they will destroy team performance.

Here's one of the most important aspects of this entire process. The key factor in leaving behind a legacy of safety that will last long after you move on is hiring winners. When complaining Joe retires, replace him with a winner. When any person leaves, for that matter, replace that person with a winner. When your division expands, fill every position with winners.

I learned this concept many years ago from Cedar River Paper Company while I was living in Cedar Rapids, Iowa. My friend John was the HR manager. He shared with me the fact that they hire for personality, not technical skills. They felt they could teach people those skills, but they couldn't teach out bad behaviors associated with bad attitudes. What an epiphany! We don't have to settle for poor attitudes. By agreeing on what personality traits we want in the ideal candidate, adding it to the job description, formulating interview questions to determine if the prospective candidate has those skills, and hiring the one who does, voila: you now have a strong candidate to join the team. It's a beautiful thing.

The company/employee relationship is a partnership. The prospective new employee walks into an interview wanting to know exactly what he or she can expect from the company. So why can't the company know what it can expect from the possible new employee? Every industry should want to hire winners who automatically have a safety conscience. We can teach them the rules and safe work practices. We can't continue to bring in the industry cowboys, rough riders, or risk-takers. Doesn't it make sense to try to bring new employees into the company who already exhibit the behaviors we want in our team members?

What are the traits of a winner? For this question, feel free to go back and review the winner list and the champion list. Another great tool to use in developing some of your new interview questions is the list of core skills for employees I've included in chapter 3. Some other examples of good traits are leadership, teamwork, commitment to task, communication, interaction, safety, respecting diversity, and the list goes on. You and your team can discuss the behaviors you need for the team to be successful. Once you and your team agree on select traits, get human resources to help you form questions around those attributes. The goal is to allow the team to describe the ideal candidate and then make up interview questions based on the personality traits the team identified. For example, we wanted to hire people who have a natural inclination toward safety and accountability, so we asked the following questions:

- Share with us a time when you demonstrated accountability for your actions.

- "Give us an example of a time when you saw someone doing an unsafe act—what did you do?"

- "Describe a time when you were faced with following a safety rule or taking a shortcut—what did you do?"

- "Describe a time when you went the extra mile for a team member—what was the situation, and what was the outcome?"

My team used this question philosophy and hired eleven of the most fantastic guys to join our team—guys who went on to be superstars for the region and the company.

Always hire winners because winners are naturally inclined to accept and support an encouraging team culture focused on love, trust, commitment, and belief; winners meet the expectations of their team leaders; winners believe in themselves and bring energy to the team; winners place higher expectations on themselves; winners emulate their leaders; winners respond to opportunities; and they will develop into amazing teammates with all the winning qualities that will help take your division and your company to a higher level of performance.

On the following page is an example of a winner who served my Kinston Construction team. This e-mail from an actual safety chairman was forwarded to me by one of its original recipients. It demonstrates what winners can accomplish when working in an encouraging team culture. The author of the letter, Brian Moore, rose to the challenge of taking his team to a high level of safety performance. He demonstrates the kind of leadership that's needed throughout the power industry.

Read this letter to your team and ask them what they hear in Brian's message. They should hear love, trust, commitment, belief, encouragement, expectations, concern, respect, appreciation, and passion.

TESTIMONY OF A SAFETY LEADER

Good morning Kinston Construction Crew,

When you receive this email, we will have been 206 days accident and injury free this year. As I have said in the past, this was not accomplished by accident. It was accomplished by total commitment and focus on safety by everyone. I would like to take this time to thank everyone for the respect and hard work that was shown during my time as PIC. It makes the job of the PIC a lot easier when you have employees that work as safe and as hard as the Kinston Construction Crew.

As we continue through the year, we don't need to overlook the small things. If we continue to work as we have, we will finish the year accident and injury free. On July 26th, we will be having a recognition dinner to celebrate our second quarter of being accident and injury free. As your safety chairman, I ask that you continue your focus on safety, focus on the job at hand, and utilizing the "what-if" culture. I would also like to welcome Brent Whitford to the Kinston Construction Crew.

Thanks, Brian Moore, Kinston L&S

Challenge your team to take this type of leadership role and to take ownership of the overall safety of their team. Ask them to list some next steps to get them from where they are to where they want to be.

ARE YOU WILLING TO PAY THE PRICE?

CHAPTER 6: ARE YOU WILLING TO PAY THE PRICE?

"There's only one way to succeed in anything, and that is to give it everything. I do, and I demand that my players do."

—Vince Lombardi

I've seen the horrific injuries that result when linemen make contact with a live power line or experience a phase flashing and major equipment failure. I've seen linemen who have lost limbs or become disfigured for life because of taking dangerous shortcuts, failing to follow the correct (and safe) procedures, and not wearing all their personal protection equipment. The effects of serious injuries result not only in lost time at work but also have major personal implications. For example, if a lineman who was not wearing the proper gloves accidently touched a live electric wire and seriously burns or loses his hands, much of what he does at home also comes to a halt. He can't mow the lawn or change the air filters. He can no longer coach softball, participate in the bowling league, go fishing with his friends, or even pick up a gallon of milk from the grocery store. These examples are only from the electric utility industry; I'm sure you can list just as many from your industry. Life changes after a serious event—sometimes forever.

Achieving a higher level of safety performance in any organization requires courageous leaders who are willing to work passionately for change. When you dare to have a big vision and are committed to reaching it, amazing things will start to happen all around you. The team culture will change, individual expectations will rise, those exhibiting bad behaviors will adapt or fall away, and winners will begin to fill the ranks of your team. It happened all because you choose to step up your leadership game and make it happen. It happened because you cared enough about your coworkers to do everything necessary to make sure they got home safely to their families after a productive and successful day at work.

Throughout my career in the power industry, whenever I took over a new group, my vision was always the same: ZERO accident and injuries. Whenever I was accused of setting too lofty a goal, I recalled the words of renowned Renaissance artist, architect, and poet Michelangelo, a man who dared to aim high: "The greatest danger for most of us lies not in setting our aim too high and falling short but in setting our aim too low and achieving our mark."

Another quote I love comes from my friend, Kenston Griffin, owner of Dream Builders Communication, Inc: "If better is possible, then good is no longer an option." So for me, aiming for ZERO was the only option. You may have a different vision for your team, which is just fine with me, although I urge you to heed the words of the great Michelangelo and Kenston.

Here's the thing, though—if you don't have a vision for your team, then other people are going to come up with one, and it likely won't be the vision you want. By not expounding a vision that your team can rally around and support wholeheartedly, you risk letting in those characteristics that are inherent in us as human beings—our desire to dominate each other, to put each other down, to war against each other, or to establish in-crowds and cliques—will emerge and ultimately fill the void where your vision for your team (the one that would have taken your team to a higher level of safety performance just by aiming for it) should have been. Don't let that happen. Develop a vision worthy of your team, and then spread the word any way you can.

When you use your leadership skills to get your team focused on that vision, you've taken the first step to establishing a workplace that is so awesome that people want to come to work every day. As an encouraging team culture begins to evolve, not only do people want to come to work, they want to come and do and be their best. They want to contribute their creative ideas to help others be their best. They want to help each other do their jobs better while staying safer. Achieving a higher level of safety performance is just a by-product of a great team culture.

As an encouraging team culture begins to evolve, not only do people want to come to work, they want to come and do and be their best.

But as a leader, your responsibilities go beyond keeping your teammates safe. You have productivity goals. You have customer-service goals. You need to make things happen in all aspects of your department or division or company. Guess what? When you create a great team culture, your team will get engaged and help you make all those things happen, too. They will come up with better ways of doing certain tasks that you never thought of. (After all, they are the ones doing those tasks every day.) When you know that other safety leaders and teammates are carrying your safety message far and wide, emulating your exact message every day, you have more time to focus on that sudden equipment failure problem that's plaguing one division or to organize a team to research and recommend the best way to upgrade the technology for a division. Your teammates step up across the board to help you get things done because you were willing to step up as a leader and pay the price to change the team culture. It's a beautiful thing!

CONCLUSION

"Whether you think you can, or whether you think you can't—you're right."

—Henry Ford, American industrialist and founder of the Ford Motor Company

ATTITUDE OF A SERVANT LEADER, C. GENE WILKES AND JOHN C. MAXWELL

Placing others' needs before one's own.

Committing yourself to doing concrete things to meet the needs of others.

Giving with no strings attached.

Seeking to achieve great goals more than great personal gain.

Rather than being intimidated by others' potential, the servant leader rejoices in their growth, development, and achievements.

To lead others, one must serve others.[1,2]

---

1   John Maxwell, *Becoming a Person of Influence* (Nashville, Tennessee: Thomas Nelson, Inc., 1997).

2   C. Gene Wilkes, *Jesus on Leadership* (Lifeway Press, 1998).

I love the halftime speech from the movie *Friday Night Lights*, which stars Billy Bob Thornton as the coach of a high school football team playing in a very important game. During his halftime speech, he explains to the team what is meant by being perfect:

> *It's about you and your relationships to yourself, your family, your friends. Being perfect is about being able to look your friends in the eye and know that you didn't let them down because you told them the truth, and*

*that truth is that you did everything that you could—
there wasn't one more thing that you coulda done. Can
you live in that moment, as best you can, with clear
eyes and love in your heart—with joy in your heart. If
you can do that gentleman, then you're perfect.*[3]

This is exactly the perfection you want your team to have.

Every team member doing everything they can for each other, not holding back on anything. This is the point where good things happen.

I saw that a teammate's ladder wasn't secured properly, so I stopped him from climbing onto the roof and helped him get it done. I noted that his favorite tool was duct-taped together, so I requisitioned a new one. I saw that a teammate was having difficulty lifting a large spool of cabling, so I lent a hand.

When your workplace transitions to a place with an encouraging team culture focused on love, trust, commitment, and belief, the positive attitudes, the engagement, the striving for perfection, and the new creativity will all spill over into your teammates' homes and communities. Suddenly you're hearing about how fathers are more engaged with their children, and volunteerism in the community skyrockets. Team members become great givers, on and off the job.

---

3   "Coach Gaines on Being Perfect," *Friday Night Lights*. Directed by Peter Berg, 2004.

ZERO ACCIDENTS & INJURIES

This entire process began with leadership, so I think it's appropriate to end with a few more words about leadership.

Leadership isn't about always being the smartest one in the room. It isn't about knowing everything about everything. That's absolutely what it isn't about.

Leadership is about serving the team.

Throughout my career in the power industry, I've been called a great leader on many occasions. What that means to me is that I was a great servant; that I had the privilege of serving my coworkers; that I genuinely loved them and their families. It means that I was willing to do everything I could to help them be the best they could be; that I praised them, found their strengths, and empowered them to be their brothers' and sisters' keepers. I like to think that my service resulted in saving a team member from serious injury and maybe even resulted in saving a few lives along the way because I had the courage as a leader to step up, speak up, and follow up when things weren't right. I helped teammates get the promotions they wanted and helped get them into positions where they could be the most successful. I helped teammates get into colleges. When some of them doubted themselves or that they could make the grade, I believed in them first (just like the first day I met them) and then stepped back as they proved me right.

I went into the classrooms of team members' children and made presentations. I wrote letters of recommendation to help teammates' children get into the colleges of their choice. I offered my counseling to any teammate who had a crisis.

When my last day in the industry or my life arrives, I won't be able to say that I've done everything right, but I can say that I've risen to be the kind of servant leader who chose to build people up rather than tear them down. I will be assured those teammates I believed in would step up and carry on the legacy of achieving a higher level of safety performance. I guess I did a few things right.

Now it's your turn.

BOOKS:

- *Becoming a Person of Influence: How to Positively Impact the Lives of Others*, by John C. Maxwell and Jim Dornan

- *Developing the Leaders Around You: How to Help Others Reach Their Full Potential*, by John C. Maxwell

- *The Leadership Challenge: How to Make Extraordinary Things Happen in Organizations*, by Barry Posner and James M. Kouzes

- *Bringing Out the Best in People*, by Aubrey Daniels

- *The New One Minute Manager*, by Ken Blanchard, PhD, and Spencer Johnson, MD

- *Emotional Intelligence: Why It Can Matter More Than IQ,* by Daniel Goleman

VIDEO CLIPS I SHOWED TO MY TEAMS TO INSPIRE THEIR BEST PERFORMANCE— THEY WILL WORK FOR YOU, TOO:

- *Friday Night Lights*: Understanding "Being Perfect"

- "Do Right," "Do Right II," and "If Enough People Care" videos featuring Lou Holtz

- "Gung Ho" video featuring Ken Blanchard and Sheldon Bowles